COLORING BOOK

This book belongs to:

....

Welcome to Trailblazers for Change: Mina and Myron Learn About Historic Firsts!

Hello all,

You will be going on this exciting journey with Mina and Myron as they learn about some amazing leaders who made history. These individuals broke barriers and paved the way for future generations.

In 1993 I had the honor of meeting Shirley Chisholm while I was a student at Morris Brown College. Her courage and determination to make change happen left a lasting impact on me, and she continues to be my inspiration for this coloring book.

I hope this book encourages you to dream big, believe in your own voice, and be a part of making history too! Enjoy coloring, learning, and exploring the stories of these amazing trailblazers.

Warmly,
Kimberly A. Morrow

Kimberly A. Morrow, my daughter Kamaria, and Shirley Chisholm

Morris Brown College, 1993

Dedication

This coloring book is dedicated to my three children Kamaria, Brandan, and Brian Jr.

ISBN: 979-8-218-51513-3

K.A.M.'S PUBLISHING CO. LLC
3651 S. La Brea STE 511
Los Angeles, CA, 90008

WWW.KIMAMORROW.COM

K.A.M'S PUBLISHING COMPANY.LLC

Eight-year-old Mina sat at the kitchen table coloring while her brother Myron read his favorite book. Their grandmother was sipping tea when something on the front page of the newspaper caught Mina's attention.

"Grandma, what are they saying about Kamala Harris?" Mina asked, pointing to the headline.

Their grandma smiled set down the paper and replied, "It's all about her running for President now. Myron looked up and said, "I thought Joe Biden was President". Their Grandma looked, and responded, "he is the president, but he has decided not to run for re-election." Kamala Harris is running and she is not the first woman or Black woman to run, she said. She asked Mina and Myron, "Would you like to learn more about her and some other important people who made history".

B-O-R-I-N-G!, Myron, said and went back to reading his book. Mina, yelled," That's not boring!" She smiled at her grandma and said, "Yes please tell us about Kamala Harris".

Grandma pulled out a photo album and opened it to a page with a picture of a smiling woman. She pointed to the picture and said. "This is Shirley Chisholm. she was the first Black woman elected to the U.S. Congress and the first Black woman to run for president. She ran for the Democratic nomination in 1972. even though many people told her she couldn't do it."

Mina's eyes widened. "Why did they say she couldn't?" Myron who sat looking bored looked up and asked. "Grandma. why did they say that?"

"Because she was a Black woman" their grandma explained. She added. Shirley Chisholm believed that everyone should have a chance to lead no matter what they looked like or where they came from. She told them her famous saying was "Unbought and Unbossed. " What does that mean?". Mina asked. Her grandma said. "It means she didn't let anyone tell her what to do."

Mina smiled and said, "She sounds awesome!"

"She was," Grandma smiled and nodded. "She opened doors for others to follow, like Jesse Jackson."

Their grandma turned the page to show a photo of a man with a kind face. "Jesse Jackson was a civil rights leader who also ran for the Democratic Presidential nomination. He ran in 1984 and 1988, and he did something amazing. Mina and Myron asked at the same time, "What did he do?" He brought together people of all races and backgrounds to support him. He also showed us that even someone who grew up poor in Greenville, South Carolina could dream big and make a difference."

Myron thought for a moment and then said. "So he was like Shirley Chisholm?"

His grandma looked at him with a grin and said. "Yes. he was!" Jesse Jackson continued the work Shirley Chisholm started and inspired even more people to believe in themselves.

Next. Grandma turned the page and pointed to a picture of a man with a big smile. standing in front of the White House. "Do you know who this man is". They both looked at each other and said together. "Barack Obama!" Mina then replied. "he was the first Black President." Myron chimed in. "Mama and Daddy talk about him all the time". Grandma said smiling at Mina and Myron. "I'm so glad to hear you've been listening". He became the first Black President of the United States in 2008. Just like Shirley Chisholm and Jesse Jackson. he also ran as a Democrat. He believed in hope and change and inspired millions of people to get involved in making the world better."

Mina says happily, "Our teacher has shown us videos of his speeches." Myron chimes in, "Yeah, I like the one when he drops the mic after his speech". Grandma looks at the twins and says proudly, "Barack Obama made history by showing us that it was possible for someone like him—like us—to lead the country".

Mina imagines her and Myron standing in front of the Whitehouse dressed as young presidents.

Grandma then turned to another page and showed a picture of a woman who looked like a leader. The twins both shouted. "That's Hillary Clinton!"

"Yes, it is", their grandma replied. She asked them to tell her what they knew about her. "She was married to President Clinton", Myron said. "She was a senator", Mina said. Grandma added, that in 2016, she became the first woman to receive the Democratic nomination for President. She showed that women can compete on the highest levels in politics.

Mina looked at the picture in awe. "Wow, Grandma, she must have been really strong!"

"She is still strong," Grandma said with a nod. She is another person who has paved the way for Kamala Harris.

Finally, Grandma turned to a picture of Kamala Harris. "And now we have Kamala Harris. She was the first woman and the first Black and South Asian woman to become Vice President. Now, she's running for President, and she stands on the shoulders of all those who came before her."

Mina looked at the photos of Shirley Chisholm, Jesse Jackson, Barack Obama, Hillary Clinton, and Kamala Harris. "So, Shirley Chisholm opened the door for Jesse Jackson who opened the door for Barack Obama, who opened the door for Hillary Clinton and now the door is opened to Kamala Harris who could become President" Myron asks.

"Exactly!" Grandma said, giving Mina and Myron a big hug. "Each of them helped pave the way for the next, making it easier for more people to dream big and achieve their goals. Do you know what that means?"

Mina shook her head. "What does it mean, Grandma?"

"It means that one day, you could be President too," Grandma said with a smile. "Or whatever you want to be. They showed us that anything is possible if you believe in yourself and work hard."

Mina smiled, feeling inspired. "I'm going to learn more about them and tell my friends at school. Maybe we can all be like them one day."

Grandma kissed the top of Mina's head. "I'm sure you will, sweetheart. The future is wide open, and you have the power to shape it, just like Shirley Chisholm, Jesse Jackson, Barack Obama, Hillary Clinton, and Kamala Harris." They all go back to the living room where Grandma continues to read with Mina and Myron listening to her.

Road to the Whitehouse

Help Mina and Myron find their way to the Whitehouse to meet Vice-President Kamala Harris.

FUTURE ME

Draw a picture of your future self as president, doctor, firefighter, teacher, or inventor.

Wordsearch

Create your own word search using the names and keywords from the story.

Thank You

FOR YOUR PURCHASE!

Please leave a review and let me know how you much you enjoyed the coloring pages. You may order the coloring book directly from my website www.kimamorrow.com or by visiting Amazon.com

Contact Me

To book me as as speaker or Vision Board Workshop facilitator.

WWW.KIMAMORROW.COM

kim.kamspub@gmail.com